50 Cooking on Charcoal Recipes

By: Kelly Johnson

Table of Contents

- Grilled Ribeye Steak
- Charcoal Grilled Chicken Thighs
- BBQ Pork Ribs
- Grilled Corn on the Cob
- Charcoal-Grilled Burgers
- Smoked Brisket
- Grilled Portobello Mushrooms
- Grilled Pineapple Slices
- Charcoal-Grilled Hot Dogs
- BBQ Chicken Wings
- Grilled Lamb Chops
- Grilled Zucchini and Squash
- Grilled Shrimp Skewers
- Smoked Sausage Links
- Grilled T-Bone Steak
- Charcoal-Grilled Salmon Fillets
- Grilled Vegetable Kabobs

- Smoked Pulled Pork
- Grilled Jalapeño Poppers
- Charcoal-Grilled Pizza
- Cedar Plank Salmon
- Grilled Eggplant Slices
- Charcoal BBQ Chicken Drumsticks
- Grilled Asparagus Bundles
- Charcoal-Smoked Turkey Breast
- Grilled Peaches with Honey
- Grilled Flat Iron Steak
- Grilled Cheese-Stuffed Burgers
- Grilled Chicken Kebabs
- Smoked Pork Tenderloin
- Charcoal-Grilled Lobster Tails
- Grilled Garlic Bread
- Grilled Halloumi Cheese
- Smoked Beef Ribs
- Grilled BBQ Meatballs
- Grilled Romaine Caesar Salad

- Charcoal-Grilled Tuna Steaks
- Smoked Mac and Cheese
- Grilled Bacon-Wrapped Scallops
- Grilled Chicken Fajitas
- Charcoal-Grilled Bratwurst
- Smoked Stuffed Bell Peppers
- Grilled Pineapple Chicken
- Grilled Steak Tacos
- BBQ Glazed Chicken Breasts
- Charcoal-Roasted Potatoes
- Grilled Pork Chops
- Smoked Chicken Wings
- Grilled Onion Slices
- Grilled BBQ Tofu

Grilled Ribeye Steak

Ingredients:

- 2 ribeye steaks (1–1.5 inches thick)
- 2 tbsp olive oil
- Salt and freshly cracked black pepper
- Optional: garlic powder, rosemary, or steak seasoning

Instructions:

1. Let steaks come to room temperature (about 30 minutes).
2. Brush both sides with olive oil and season generously with salt and pepper.
3. Preheat grill to high heat (450–500°F).
4. Grill steaks 4–5 minutes per side for medium-rare, adjusting time for preferred doneness.
5. Rest for 5 minutes before slicing to retain juices.

Charcoal Grilled Chicken Thighs

Ingredients:

- 6 bone-in, skin-on chicken thighs
- 2 tbsp olive oil
- 2 tsp smoked paprika
- 1 tsp garlic powder
- Salt and pepper to taste

Instructions:

1. Rub thighs with olive oil and seasonings.
2. Prepare charcoal grill for indirect heat.
3. Grill chicken skin-side down over indirect heat for 25–30 minutes, then sear over direct heat 2–3 minutes per side.
4. Internal temp should reach 165°F. Let rest 5 minutes before serving.

BBQ Pork Ribs

Ingredients:

- 1 rack baby back ribs
- Your favorite dry rub (paprika, garlic, onion powder, salt, pepper)
- Sugar-free BBQ sauce (optional)

Instructions:

1. Remove membrane from ribs and coat with dry rub.
2. Wrap in foil and grill over indirect heat at 300°F for 2–2.5 hours.
3. Unwrap, brush with BBQ sauce, and grill over direct heat for 10–15 minutes until caramelized.
4. Rest before slicing.

Grilled Corn on the Cob

Ingredients:

- 4 ears of corn, husks removed
- 2 tbsp butter, melted
- Salt and pepper

Instructions:

1. Brush corn with melted butter and season.
2. Grill over medium heat, turning every few minutes, for about 10–15 minutes until slightly charred.
3. Serve hot with extra butter if desired.

Charcoal-Grilled Burgers

Ingredients:

- 1.5 lbs ground beef (80/20)
- Salt and pepper
- Optional: cheese, lettuce, tomato, onions, keto buns or lettuce wraps

Instructions:

1. Form into 4 patties and season generously.
2. Grill over direct heat 4–5 minutes per side for medium doneness.
3. Add cheese in the last minute if using.
4. Serve as desired.

Smoked Brisket

Ingredients:

- 4–5 lb beef brisket
- Your favorite rub (salt, pepper, garlic, paprika)
- Wood chips for smoking (oak or hickory)

Instructions:

1. Rub brisket generously and let sit for 1 hour.
2. Set grill or smoker for indirect heat at 225–250°F, add wood chips.
3. Smoke for 6–8 hours until internal temp reaches ~195–203°F.
4. Let rest wrapped in foil for 1 hour before slicing.

Grilled Portobello Mushrooms

Ingredients:

- 4 large portobello caps
- 2 tbsp olive oil
- 1 tsp balsamic vinegar
- Salt, pepper, garlic powder

Instructions:

1. Brush mushrooms with oil and vinegar, season.
2. Grill over medium heat for 4–5 minutes per side until tender.
3. Serve as a side or meat substitute.

Grilled Pineapple Slices

Ingredients:

- 1 fresh pineapple, sliced into rings
- 1 tbsp melted butter
- Optional: cinnamon or chili powder for a twist

Instructions:

1. Brush pineapple with butter and season if desired.
2. Grill over medium heat 2–3 minutes per side until caramelized.
3. Serve warm as a side or dessert.

Charcoal-Grilled Hot Dogs

Ingredients:

- 8 beef hot dogs

- Optional: buns, mustard, onions, relish, or keto toppings

Instructions:

1. Grill hot dogs over direct heat for 5–7 minutes, turning occasionally until charred.

2. Serve immediately with desired toppings.

BBQ Chicken Wings

Ingredients:

- 2 lbs chicken wings
- Salt and pepper
- 1 tbsp olive oil
- 1/2 cup sugar-free BBQ sauce

Instructions:

1. Toss wings in olive oil, salt, and pepper.
2. Grill over medium heat for 20–25 minutes, turning occasionally.
3. During the last 5 minutes, brush with BBQ sauce and continue grilling until caramelized.
4. Let rest a few minutes before serving.

Grilled Lamb Chops

Ingredients:

- 8 lamb chops
- 2 tbsp olive oil
- 1 tbsp chopped rosemary
- 2 garlic cloves, minced
- Salt and pepper

Instructions:

1. Marinate lamb chops with olive oil, garlic, rosemary, salt, and pepper for at least 30 minutes.
2. Grill over high heat for 3–4 minutes per side for medium-rare.
3. Let rest 5 minutes before serving.

Grilled Zucchini and Squash

Ingredients:

- 2 zucchini, 2 yellow squash, sliced lengthwise
- 2 tbsp olive oil
- Salt, pepper, garlic powder

Instructions:

1. Brush slices with olive oil and season.
2. Grill over medium-high heat for 3–4 minutes per side until tender and lightly charred.
3. Serve warm or at room temperature.

Grilled Shrimp Skewers

Ingredients:

- 1 lb large shrimp, peeled and deveined
- 2 tbsp olive oil
- Juice of 1 lemon
- 2 cloves garlic, minced
- Salt, pepper, paprika

Instructions:

1. Toss shrimp with olive oil, lemon juice, garlic, and seasoning.
2. Thread onto skewers.
3. Grill over medium-high heat for 2–3 minutes per side until pink and opaque.
4. Serve immediately.

Smoked Sausage Links

Ingredients:

- 1 lb smoked sausage links (kielbasa or andouille)

Instructions:

1. Place sausage links on indirect heat side of a preheated grill at 225–250°F.
2. Smoke for 1–1.5 hours, turning once, until heated through and lightly browned.
3. Slice and serve.

Grilled T-Bone Steak

Ingredients:

- 2 T-bone steaks
- Salt, pepper, garlic powder
- 1 tbsp olive oil

Instructions:

1. Rub steaks with oil and season generously.
2. Grill over high heat for 4–5 minutes per side for medium-rare.
3. Rest for 5–10 minutes before slicing.

Charcoal-Grilled Salmon Fillets

Ingredients:

- 4 salmon fillets (skin-on)
- 2 tbsp olive oil
- 1 tbsp lemon juice
- Salt, pepper, dill or garlic powder

Instructions:

1. Brush salmon with olive oil, lemon juice, and seasonings.
2. Grill skin-side down over indirect heat for 6–8 minutes.
3. Flip carefully and cook 2–3 minutes more.
4. Serve with lemon wedges.

Grilled Vegetable Kabobs

Ingredients:

- 1 red bell pepper, 1 zucchini, 1 red onion, mushrooms, cherry tomatoes
- 2 tbsp olive oil
- Salt, pepper, Italian herbs

Instructions:

1. Cut vegetables into chunks and toss with oil and seasoning.
2. Thread onto skewers.
3. Grill over medium-high heat, turning often, for 10–12 minutes until tender.
4. Serve hot or warm.

Smoked Pulled Pork

Ingredients:

- 4–5 lb pork shoulder (Boston butt)
- 1/4 cup dry rub (paprika, salt, pepper, garlic, cayenne)
- Wood chips (hickory or apple)

Instructions:

1. Rub pork shoulder and let sit overnight in fridge.
2. Smoke at 225°F for 8–10 hours, until internal temp hits ~200°F.
3. Let rest for 30 minutes, then shred with forks.
4. Serve with keto-friendly BBQ sauce if desired.

Grilled Jalapeño Poppers

Ingredients:

- 8 jalapeños, halved and seeded
- 4 oz cream cheese
- 1/2 cup shredded cheddar
- 8 slices bacon, cut in half

Instructions:

1. Mix cream cheese and cheddar. Fill each jalapeño half with mixture.
2. Wrap each with a half slice of bacon.
3. Secure with toothpicks and grill over indirect heat for 15–20 minutes until bacon is crisp and peppers are tender.

Charcoal-Grilled Pizza

Ingredients:

- 1 low-carb pizza crust (or fathead dough)
- 1/4 cup tomato sauce (no sugar added)
- 1 cup mozzarella
- Toppings: pepperoni, olives, mushrooms, etc.

Instructions:

1. Preheat grill for indirect heat.
2. Grill crust for 2–3 minutes per side.
3. Add sauce, cheese, and toppings.
4. Return to grill with lid closed until cheese melts (5–7 minutes).

Cedar Plank Salmon

Ingredients:

- 4 salmon fillets
- 1 cedar plank (soaked in water for 1 hour)
- 2 tbsp olive oil
- Lemon slices, fresh dill, salt, pepper

Instructions:

1. Season salmon and place on soaked cedar plank.
2. Grill over indirect heat with lid closed for 15–20 minutes.
3. Salmon is done when it flakes easily and reaches 145°F internally.

Grilled Eggplant Slices

Ingredients:

- 1 large eggplant, sliced into ½-inch rounds
- Olive oil, salt, pepper, garlic powder

Instructions:

1. Brush slices with oil and season.
2. Grill over medium heat for 3–4 minutes per side until soft and lightly charred.
3. Serve warm, optionally with feta or balsamic drizzle.

Charcoal BBQ Chicken Drumsticks

Ingredients:

- 8 chicken drumsticks
- 2 tbsp olive oil
- Salt, pepper, paprika
- 1/2 cup sugar-free BBQ sauce

Instructions:

1. Coat drumsticks in oil and seasonings.
2. Grill over indirect heat for 30–35 minutes, turning occasionally.
3. In final 5 minutes, baste with BBQ sauce and grill over direct heat to char.
4. Internal temp should reach 165°F.

Grilled Asparagus Bundles

Ingredients:

- 1 bunch asparagus, trimmed
- 6 slices prosciutto or bacon
- Olive oil, pepper

Instructions:

1. Wrap 4–5 spears with a slice of prosciutto or bacon.
2. Brush with olive oil and season.
3. Grill over medium-high heat for 5–7 minutes, turning once, until crisp-tender.

Charcoal-Smoked Turkey Breast

Ingredients:

- 3–4 lb boneless turkey breast
- 2 tbsp olive oil
- Dry rub: salt, pepper, paprika, garlic powder
- Wood chips for smoke (apple or cherry)

Instructions:

1. Rub turkey breast and let sit for 30 minutes.
2. Smoke at 250°F over indirect heat for 2–3 hours, until internal temp reaches 165°F.
3. Let rest 15 minutes before slicing.

Grilled Peaches with Honey

Ingredients:

- 4 ripe peaches, halved and pitted
- 1 tbsp melted butter
- 1 tbsp honey (or sugar-free substitute)

Instructions:

1. Brush peaches with butter.
2. Grill cut side down for 3–4 minutes until caramelized.
3. Drizzle with honey before serving.

Grilled Flat Iron Steak

Ingredients:

- 1.5–2 lb flat iron steak
- Salt, pepper, garlic powder
- 1 tbsp olive oil

Instructions:

1. Season steak and let sit at room temp 30 minutes.
2. Grill over high heat for 4–5 minutes per side for medium-rare.
3. Let rest 5 minutes, then slice against the grain.

Grilled Cheese-Stuffed Burgers

Ingredients:

- 1.5 lbs ground beef
- Salt, pepper, garlic powder
- 4 oz cheddar or mozzarella, cubed or shredded
- Burger buns or lettuce wraps (optional)

Instructions:

1. Form 8 thin burger patties.
2. Place cheese in the center of 4, then top with remaining patties and seal edges.
3. Season and grill over medium-high heat for 5–6 minutes per side, until cooked through and cheese is melted.
4. Let rest briefly before serving.

Grilled Chicken Kebabs

Ingredients:

- 1.5 lbs chicken breast, cubed
- 2 bell peppers, 1 red onion, cubed
- Marinade: 2 tbsp olive oil, 1 tbsp lemon juice, garlic, salt, pepper

Instructions:

1. Marinate chicken and veggies for 30+ minutes.
2. Thread onto skewers, alternating ingredients.
3. Grill over medium-high heat for 10–12 minutes, turning occasionally, until chicken is cooked through.

Smoked Pork Tenderloin

Ingredients:

- 1 pork tenderloin
- 1 tbsp olive oil
- Dry rub: paprika, garlic powder, salt, pepper
- Wood chips for smoke

Instructions:

1. Rub tenderloin and let rest at room temp for 30 minutes.
2. Smoke at 225°F for 1.5–2 hours until internal temp reaches 145°F.
3. Let rest 10 minutes before slicing.

Charcoal-Grilled Lobster Tails

Ingredients:

- 4 lobster tails
- 1/4 cup melted butter
- 2 cloves garlic, minced
- Lemon wedges

Instructions:

1. Cut shells to expose meat, brush with garlic butter.
2. Grill shell-side down over medium heat for 8–10 minutes until meat is opaque.
3. Serve with extra melted butter and lemon.

Grilled Garlic Bread

Ingredients:

- Low-carb or keto bread slices
- 3 tbsp butter
- 2 cloves garlic, minced
- Chopped parsley (optional)

Instructions:

1. Mix butter and garlic; spread on bread slices.
2. Grill over medium heat for 1–2 minutes per side until toasted.
3. Sprinkle with parsley before serving.

Grilled Halloumi Cheese

Ingredients:

- 8 oz halloumi cheese, sliced into ½" thick pieces
- Olive oil

Instructions:

1. Brush slices with olive oil.
2. Grill over medium heat for 1–2 minutes per side until golden and grill-marked.
3. Serve warm, optionally with lemon juice or herbs.

Smoked Beef Ribs

Ingredients:

- 2–3 lbs beef short ribs
- 2 tbsp dry rub (salt, pepper, paprika, garlic powder)
- Wood chips (oak or hickory)

Instructions:

1. Apply dry rub to ribs and let sit for 30 minutes.
2. Smoke at 250°F for 4–6 hours, until meat is tender and internal temp reaches ~200°F.
3. Rest 20 minutes before slicing.

Grilled BBQ Meatballs

Ingredients:

- 1.5 lbs ground beef
- 1 egg, 1/4 cup almond flour
- Salt, pepper, onion powder
- 1/2 cup sugar-free BBQ sauce

Instructions:

1. Mix ingredients, roll into 1.5-inch balls.
2. Skewer or place on grill-safe tray.
3. Grill over medium heat for 10–12 minutes, brushing with BBQ sauce during the last 5 minutes.

Grilled Romaine Caesar Salad

Ingredients:

- 2 romaine hearts, halved lengthwise
- Olive oil, salt, pepper
- Caesar dressing, shaved parmesan, optional anchovies

Instructions:

1. Brush romaine with olive oil, season.
2. Grill cut-side down over high heat for 1–2 minutes until lightly charred.
3. Serve drizzled with Caesar dressing and parmesan.

Charcoal-Grilled Tuna Steaks

Ingredients:

- 4 tuna steaks (1-inch thick)
- 2 tbsp olive oil
- 1 tbsp soy sauce or coconut aminos
- 1 tsp lemon juice
- Salt and pepper

Instructions:

1. Marinate tuna in olive oil, soy sauce, and lemon juice for 20 minutes.
2. Grill over high heat for 2–3 minutes per side for medium-rare, or longer if preferred.
3. Serve immediately with a squeeze of fresh lemon.

Smoked Mac and Cheese

Ingredients:

- 2 cups shredded cheddar
- 1 cup shredded mozzarella
- 2 cups cooked low-carb pasta or cauliflower florets
- 1/2 cup heavy cream
- 2 tbsp butter
- Salt, pepper, paprika

Instructions:

1. Mix all ingredients in a cast-iron skillet or foil pan.
2. Smoke at 225–250°F for 1–1.5 hours until bubbly and golden on top.
3. Stir halfway through and serve hot.

Grilled Bacon-Wrapped Scallops

Ingredients:

- 12 large scallops
- 6 slices bacon, cut in half
- Toothpicks

Instructions:

1. Wrap each scallop in a half slice of bacon and secure with toothpicks.
2. Grill over medium heat for 4–5 minutes per side until bacon is crisp and scallops are opaque.
3. Optional: baste with garlic butter while grilling.

Grilled Chicken Fajitas

Ingredients:

- 1.5 lbs chicken breast, sliced
- 2 bell peppers, 1 onion, sliced
- 2 tbsp fajita seasoning
- 2 tbsp olive oil

Instructions:

1. Toss everything in seasoning and oil.
2. Grill in a basket or skewered over medium-high heat for 10–12 minutes.
3. Serve with low-carb tortillas or over lettuce.

Charcoal-Grilled Bratwurst

Ingredients:

- 6 bratwurst sausages
- 1 can beer (optional for soaking)
- Buns or lettuce wraps

Instructions:

1. Optional: simmer brats in beer for 10 minutes.
2. Grill over medium heat for 15–20 minutes, turning often until internal temp reaches 160°F.
3. Serve with mustard, sauerkraut, or grilled onions.

Smoked Stuffed Bell Peppers

Ingredients:

- 4 bell peppers, tops removed and seeded
- 1 lb ground beef or sausage
- 1/2 cup riced cauliflower
- 1/2 cup shredded cheese
- Seasonings: salt, pepper, garlic powder

Instructions:

1. Cook filling ingredients together, then stuff into peppers.
2. Smoke at 250°F for 1.5–2 hours until peppers are tender and tops are golden.
3. Optional: top with extra cheese during last 15 minutes.

Grilled Pineapple Chicken

Ingredients:

- 1.5 lbs chicken thighs or breasts
- 1/2 cup pineapple juice
- 2 tbsp soy sauce or coconut aminos
- 1 tbsp olive oil
- Sliced fresh pineapple

Instructions:

1. Marinate chicken in pineapple juice, soy, and oil for 1 hour.
2. Grill chicken and pineapple slices over medium heat for 6–8 minutes per side.
3. Serve together garnished with fresh cilantro.

Grilled Steak Tacos

Ingredients:

- 1.5 lbs flank or skirt steak
- 1 tbsp taco seasoning
- Olive oil
- Low-carb tortillas or lettuce wraps
- Toppings: avocado, salsa, sour cream, lime

Instructions:

1. Rub steak with oil and seasoning.
2. Grill over high heat for 4–5 minutes per side.
3. Rest, slice thinly, and serve in tortillas with toppings.

BBQ Glazed Chicken Breasts

Ingredients:

- 4 boneless, skinless chicken breasts
- Salt, pepper, garlic powder
- 1/2 cup sugar-free or regular BBQ sauce

Instructions:

1. Season chicken with salt, pepper, and garlic powder.
2. Grill over medium heat for 6–8 minutes per side.
3. In the last 5 minutes, brush generously with BBQ sauce and continue cooking until internal temp hits 165°F.
4. Let rest 5 minutes before serving.

Charcoal-Roasted Potatoes

Ingredients:

- 1.5 lbs baby potatoes, halved
- 2 tbsp olive oil
- Salt, pepper, rosemary or thyme

Instructions:

1. Toss potatoes in oil and seasonings.
2. Place in a foil packet or grill basket.
3. Roast over indirect heat on the grill for 30–40 minutes, shaking or flipping halfway through, until fork-tender.

Grilled Pork Chops

Ingredients:

- 4 bone-in or boneless pork chops
- Olive oil, salt, pepper, paprika, garlic powder

Instructions:

1. Brush chops with oil and season well.
2. Grill over medium-high heat for 5–6 minutes per side, or until internal temp reaches 145°F.
3. Rest for 5 minutes before serving.

Smoked Chicken Wings

Ingredients:

- 2 lbs chicken wings
- 2 tbsp dry rub (paprika, garlic powder, salt, pepper)
- Wood chips for smoke
- Optional: BBQ sauce or buffalo sauce for tossing

Instructions:

1. Coat wings with dry rub.
2. Smoke at 225°F for 1.5–2 hours until skin is crispy and internal temp is 175°F.
3. Toss in sauce if desired and serve hot.

Grilled Onion Slices

Ingredients:

- 2 large onions, sliced into ½-inch thick rings
- 1 tbsp olive oil
- Salt and pepper

Instructions:

1. Brush onion slices with oil and season.
2. Grill over medium heat for 3–4 minutes per side until softened and charred.
3. Serve as a side or topping.

Grilled BBQ Tofu

Ingredients:

- 1 block firm tofu, pressed and sliced into slabs
- 1/2 cup BBQ sauce
- Olive oil for brushing

Instructions:

1. Brush tofu with oil and grill over medium heat for 4–5 minutes per side.
2. In the last few minutes, brush with BBQ sauce and flip once more.
3. Serve hot with extra sauce if desired.

www.ingramcontent.com/pod-product-compliance
Lightning Source LLC
LaVergne TN
LVHW061950070526
838199LV00060B/4060

9798349320897